GOD,
WHERE
IS LOVE?

Books by Claire W.

God, Help Me Stop!
God, I'm Still Hurting
God, Where Is Love?
God, Help Me Create

God, Where Is Love?

Break Free from the Pain of Codependency

Claire W.

ZondervanPublishingHouse

Grand Rapids, Michigan

A Division of HarperCollinsPublishers

God, Where Is Love?
Copyright © 1989, 1993 by Claire W.

Requests for information should be addressed to:
Zondervan Publishing House
Grand Rapids, Michigan 49530

Library of Congress Cataloging-in-Publication Data

W., Claire, 1938–
    God, where is love? : break free from the pain of codependency /
Claire W.
        p. cm.
    ISBN 0-310-40071-6 (pbk.)
    1. Codependents—Religious life. 2. Codependents—Psychology.
3. Christian life—1960– I. Title.
BV4596.C57W18   1993
248.8'6—dc20
                                                            93-28013
                                                            CIP

All Scripture quotations, unless otherwise noted, are taken from the HOLY BIBLE:
NEW INTERNATIONAL VERSION®. Copyright © 1973, 1978, 1984 by
International Bible Society. Used by permission of Zondervan Publishing House. All
rights reserved.

Edited by Jan Ortiz
Cover design by PM Graphics

Printed in the United States of America

93 94 95 96 97 98 / ML / 10 9 8 7 6 5 4 3 2 1

CONTENTS

PART I

HOW DO I LEARN
TO LOVE AND
BE LOVED?

CHAPTER 1
The Problem of Codependency

Are you single and wondering how to develop a good relationship? Are you married and hoping to strengthen or salvage an existing relationship? Are you frustrated or discouraged about it all?

Most of us want to go through life with a partner. We want a mutually loving and committed relationship in which we enjoy friendship, intimacy, and sexuality. For some of us, however, this goal is difficult to achieve.

If we are codependent, we may never feel comfortable and secure in a relationship. We tell ourselves we love and are loved, but we are not convinced. We feel something is not quite right. We cannot relax. We feel that we have to work at the relationship—to fix it—to make sure it survives.

We may in fact have been through a number of unhappy relationships. Hurting others or being hurt, leaving them or being left, we may wonder at our "bad luck."

If we look back on the history of our relationships, or if we study a relationship that is currently in trouble, we may become aware of a repetitive pattern. We may be surprised at how often we have lived through the same negative experience.

For Reflection: What kind of negative pattern can I see in my relationships?

□□□

To understand the pattern of our troubled relationships, it is helpful to look first at the kinds of people we select for partners. We may be attracted to and select people with whom it is especially difficult for us to find happiness.

Sometimes this pattern of selection is very obvious. We may, for instance, be drawn to alcoholics, or people who are physically violent. Often, however, the pattern is subtle, and we have to figure out what it is that "hooks" us.

The "hook" is usually an attitude or behavior that we are familiar with. It is the same attitude or behavior we experienced with an abusive or neglectful parent. The people we are attracted to may look very different from the parent we had problems with—and they may have a very different "style." In their presence, however, we feel as we felt when we were young.

As children, we did everything we could to win that parent's love, only to fail. As adults, we struggle to rewrite our history. "At last," we think, "I will succeed. I will make this person change. I will make this person love me."

Because of our need to meet this challenge, we may be drawn to the very people who are least likely to love us in the way we want to be loved. We may seek out those who are most likely to frustrate or hurt us.

All of this happens at an unconscious level. In the process of selecting or rejecting potential partners, we are not aware of what it is we are seeking. When we find the negative signs we are looking for, we ignore them, downplay them, or we translate them into good qualities.

To see how this works, we will look at the examples of Lynn and Steve. Although Lynn and Steve are fictitious characters, they are based on a composite of real people. Their stories will be followed throughout this book to illustrate the dynamics of codependency.

□□□

LYNN: Lynn was tall and thin, with sandy-colored hair. Although not a beautiful woman, her stylish clothing and gracious manner gave her a distinctive air. She worked as Director of Admissions at a local college.

As a child, Lynn had been afraid of her father. She had also felt invisible to him. Lynn's father, a high-ranking naval officer, was away much of the time. When

he was home, he paid little attention to Lynn—unless
he was angry. Lynn couldn't remember his ever hugging
or kissing her.

Lynn's mother, although kind and gentle, was "unavailable" most of the time, and then she had died when
Lynn was twelve. Lynn's memories of her mother were
mostly of her sleeping on the couch. In later years, Lynn
learned her mother had been addicted to prescription
drugs.

As an adult, Lynn was attracted to emotionally
distant men, especially if they seemed a little dangerous.
When she met a warm or affectionate man, she usually
found him boring. Lynn met her husband, Steve, at a
party. She saw him standing alone, apart from everyone
else. He looked moody and he was drinking.

When she went up to him, Steve looked interested in
her, but he seemed to make no special effort to be
friendly. Lynn later described Steve to her friends as "his
own man, very independent and exciting." Lynn's
friends, however, found Steve to be arrogant and
withdrawn. They wondered why Lynn was dating him.

Lynn thought it was his good looks that attracted her.
She thought it was his self-confidence that appealed to
her. In reality, however, she was responding to the
similarity between Steve and her father. Because of
Steve's emotional detachment, Lynn experienced the
same need she had experienced as a child: the need to
win attention. Because of Steve's moodiness, she also
felt some of the danger she had felt in her father's
presence.

Lynn's excitement and happiness at being with him lay in the hope that she could change him—as she had never been able to change her parents—that she could get him to pay attention to her, to assure her that he would never abandon her.

None of this, however, was understood consciously. All Lynn knew was that she was "in love."

STEVE: Average in height and build, Steve often attracted attention because of his dark good looks. By his own admission, however, he was "a little rough around the edges." Although smart enough to escape the poverty of his childhood and shrewd enough to become successful in land development, he had never finished high school. What he knew, he had learned on the streets. What he had, he had earned.

When he started going with Lynn, Steve did not make any conscious connection between Lynn and his parents. Steve's father had been coarse and loud; he would curse or use sarcasm when criticizing the boy. Steve's mother had expressed her endless judgments through raised eyebrows and gentle sighs.

Lynn, however, was as critical as Steve's parents had been. Only her style, light and sophisticated, was different. The night they met at the party, she questioned the way Steve's tie went with his suit. She also criticized the food being served, the decor, and the way the hostess was dancing.

It was this attitude that "hooked" Steve. Instead of seeing it as negative and ultimately hurtful for him, he translated it into a number of positives: Lynn was "classy and had high standards."

Steve did not realize his attraction to Lynn was based on her negativity. He was not aware that with her he had the same feelings he had when he was with his parents; a need for approval, and a sense that he would never "measure up." Steve did not realize that one of the reasons he had married Lynn was to try to accomplish his childhood dream: to win his parents' approval.

When we meet someone we are attracted to, we are not consciously aware of why we are drawn to that person. We do not recognize the renewal of a childhood challenge: to get mommy and/or daddy to love us. The excitement of this challenge, the hope that we will succeed, the fear that we will fail, the revived feelings of danger, anger, hurt, and love all have a powerful effect on us. We call this effect "chemistry."

For Reflection: To what extent is my attraction to a potential partner based on childhood experiences?

Emotionally mature people seldom experience the kind of intense initial attraction described above. If they do have this kind of experience, they are apt to mistrust it. They usually shy away from people who seem to be too sexy or exciting. They gravitate toward and feel comfortable with people who might seem uninteresting to a codependent.

□ □ □

Much of our ability to love and be loved depends on

the loving—or lack of loving—we experience in childhood. We feel loved when our parents provide for us, protect us, and guide us. We feel loved when they hug us, when they listen with interest to our ideas and feelings, when they treat us with respect, and when they express trust in us.

With this kind of support and encouragement, we learn to value and love ourselves. We grow up to be independent of the approval of other people. With this independence we are enabled to love and be loved. We make healthy choices both in selecting a partner and developing a relationship.

While most parents want to be loving toward their children, many are handicapped by their own childhood experiences of abuse or neglect. Others are handicapped by circumstances such as severe poverty or illness.

If our parents are unable to be loving and supportive of us, if they withhold approval from us, we grow up with feelings of self-doubt. Rather than being independent of others, we are codependent. That is, we are dependent on others for our sense of self-worth. We may even believe we need another person for our very survival. We are not free to love because we are bound by need and fear.

For Reflection: How dependent am I on others, or on one "special" other, for my sense of self-worth?

Overcoming codependency involves breaking with the past. It involves becoming free from any negative experience in our family of origin. When we enter into a primary relationship with another person, we codependents need to leave our parents emotionally as well as physically.

Looking at Scripture: What is it that will free me to be happily married?

> For this reason a man will leave his father
> and mother and be united to his wife, and
> they will become one flesh.
>
> GENESIS 2:24

In the chapters that follow, you will learn how to leave the past behind and prepare for a happier future. It is possible to recover from codependency. It is possible to love and be loved.

CHAPTER 2
The Work of Recovery

When our relationships become strained or fail, we usually become angry and blame our partners. Or we feel guilty and blame ourselves. Sometimes we go back and forth, blaming them, then blaming ourselves.

When it comes to codependency, however, no one is to blame. Both partners act out of deep childhood needs that were never met. It is because of our history that we pick the people we do and interact with them as we do.

While we cannot change what happened in the past, we can change the way we respond to the past—and the way we respond to our present and future circumstances. We can change ourselves.

As codependents, it may be difficult for us to focus on ourselves. Our orientation is usually toward our partner—often to the point of obsession. Anxious to create, maintain, or salvage a relationship, we concentrate on changing or controlling our partner.

Our manipulation may be very subtle: using guilt, for instance; or it may be obvious: nagging or bullying. Although our methods may differ, our intent is always the same: to control the relationship by controlling the other person. We are convinced that everything would be perfect, if only the other person would do as we want.

The Sounds of Codependency

LYNN: "I think about Steve and our relationship a lot. I try to figure out what to do to make sure things are perfect. Actually, everything would be perfect if he just wouldn't work so much. He's hardly ever at home—even on weekends. And when he does come home, he brings his work with him. He's always working—or watching sports on TV. I try dressing really well or talking about things I think will interest him, but he doesn't respond. Sometimes I feel as though I don't exist. If I let him know how upset I am, he walks out of the room—or out of the house. I get scared that he's never coming back. I know he will, but I'm frightened anyway, so I just go back to trying to please him again."

STEVE: "I think Lynn's disappointed in me, that she feels she married beneath herself. Her family's upper class, her father a big-shot navy officer. I've built up my own business and I make good money, but those people look down on me. And it rubs off on Lynn. Being around her family makes Lynn really snotty and hard to please. I don't tell her how I feel about them. I just try to keep her away from them. If we could move away—

or if they would move away—we wouldn't have any problems."

□□□

It is seldom possible to change another person. It is possible, however, to change ourselves. We can change those attitudes and behaviors that keep us interacting with people in unhealthy ways.

As we saw in the previous chapter, we sometimes seek out the very people who are least willing or able to give us the love we want. At the same time, we may avoid people who would be loving toward us. If there are caring people in our lives, we may ignore or reject the kind and loving things they do or say. We may even "train" these people to treat us badly. It is possible, for instance, to elicit criticism from others simply by behaving as though we deserve it.

For Reflection: In what ways do I reject the possibility of love?

A primary relationship always reflects the state of our own emotional health. If we constantly complain about an abusive or uncaring partner, we need to ask ourselves what choices we have made to arrive at this situation. We need to understand how we contribute to the continuation of the abuse or neglect.

Looking at Scripture: How does the relationship I have with my partner mirror my own emotional health?

> "Likewise every good tree bears good
> fruit, but a bad tree bears bad fruit. A
> good tree cannot bear bad fruit, and a bad
> tree cannot bear good fruit."
>
> MATTHEW 7:17–18

In assuming responsibility for the "fruit" of our relationships, we deal with the state of our own emotional and spiritual health. We seek recovery from codependency.

□ □ □

There are a number of resources that can help us in our recovery. One of these is therapy. Therapists who specialize in codependency (sometimes called love addiction) can be particularly helpful. A good therapist will offer support as well as perspective as we explore the relationship problems that are personal and unique to us.

Another possible resource is a self-help group such as Codependents Anonymous. We learn about ourselves when we listen to others with similar problems. A strong group can also become a second "family" to us—a family in which we are supported, encouraged, and loved.

You might want to start a group using *God, Where Is Love?* as the foundation for your studies and your interaction. There is a "Guidelines for Groups" section at the back that will help you get started.

Still another effective resource is your local library or bookstore. Additional readings on codependency can usually be found in the sections devoted to adult children from alcoholic families. Although you may not have any alcoholics in your family of origin, these books apply equally well to adult children from families made dysfunctional by other addictions, compulsions, or emotional illness (e.g., overeating, gambling, sexual compulsions, workaholism).

For Reflection: Which resources will I explore to help me in my work toward recovery?

All the resources we turn to can be helpful if we allow ourselves to be directed and guided by God. He knows our past and all the secrets of our heart. He can illuminate our darkness. If we pray for insight into our problems, he will respond to our prayer.

> If any of you lacks wisdom, he should ask God, who gives generously to all without finding fault, and it will be given to him.
> JAMES 1:5

With God's help, we are less fearful of looking back into the past and less ashamed about acknowledging our current problems. With God's guidance, we can more readily benefit from the therapy, group work, or readings we pursue. With his grace, we are able to persist in our quest for understanding, healing, and growth.

□□□

Try to be patient with yourself as you work on

recovery. You are making changes in the attitudes and habits developed over a lifetime, and that will take time.

Try also to be tolerant of yourself. Work for progress, not perfection. Recovery by its very nature involves a number of setbacks or relapses. We may need to hear a new idea or practice a new behavior many times before these things become a part of us.

If we become discouraged, we may try to blame our circumstances. We may decide it is too difficult to recover because we are single—or because we are married.

Whether single or married, however, our job is the same. We work toward goals that we ourselves choose. To achieve these goals, we must be self-motivated and self-directed. No other person can do our work for us.

Being single may make it easier in some respects. As our self-esteem increases, we have the opportunity to enter into a relationship with someone who reflects our new-found state of emotional health. Since there is no history of grievances with this person, it may be easier to move forward into a healthy and loving interaction. Until we find a partner, however, our singleness means that we must practice our relationship skills on friends and family.

Being married has different advantages. Married people have a history of shared experiences that can be bonding. Most partners feel they have an investment in making their marriage work, and most want very much to regain the initial love they felt for one another. Marriage can provide a good "laboratory" for recovery, especially if your partner is supportive. However, if you are married to someone who is emotionally ill, addicted to a chemical substance, or abusive toward you, you may need to physically separate yourself from that person in order to recover.

□□□

As children and adults, most codependents live with sadness, anger, and fear. Even if we are not consciously aware of these specific feelings, we will be aware of feeling vaguely uncomfortable most of the time. Some of us turn to addictive or compulsive behaviors in order to numb ourselves to this discomfort.

When we learn about our codependency and begin our work toward recovery, we may not be able to picture what recovery will be like. Being used to discomfort, we may find it difficult to imagine feeling good most of the time.

For Reflection: What do I think recovery will be like?

Recovery will be better than you expect it to be. When you pray for God's help in your recovery, trust that his response will be greater than what you can imagine. Thank him for the miracle he will show you.

Looking at Scripture: Will God's gift of recovery be better than I can imagine?

Now to him who is able to do immeasurably more than all we ask or imagine, according to his power that is at work within us, to him be glory in the church and in Christ Jesus throughout all generations, for ever and ever! Amen.

EPHESIANS 3:20–21

CHAPTER 3
Understanding, Healing, and Growth

Becoming free from codependency involves working toward three goals. These are: understanding, healing, and growth.

Understanding is the first goal of recovery. We need to understand how our past has affected our present. We need to realize just how our childhood experiences influence us in forming and maintaining our adult relationships.

Gaining this understanding may take effort. The dynamics of codependency are sometimes subtle and hard for us to see. We are so used to our ways of thinking and interacting that they seem normal to us. We do not realize that we are playing a role in a scenario that was taught to us as children.

The scenario originates in a conscious or unconscious abuse of power on the part of a parent. The point of any scenario can usually be summed up in a phrase such as: "I'm right, you're wrong"; "I'm important, you're not"; "I'm good, you're bad"; "I'm strong, you're weak"; "I don't need you, you need me."

As we saw in the previous chapter, we usually manage to pick a partner who knows the same scenario we do. This creates in our adult relationships the same inequality and abuse of power that existed in our family of origin.

Regardless of whether we choose to play the parent, good guy role, or the child, bad guy role, we are involved in a tremendous struggle for power and control. Because we continue to feel the vulnerability we felt as children, we continue the struggle to avoid the possibility of being hurt, rejected, or abandoned.

For Reflection: What is the scenario from childhood that I perpetuate in my adult relationships?

□□□

Because our partner knows the same scenario we do, the roles can sometimes be switched. Both Lynn and Steve knew the scenario called "I don't need you, you need me." Lynn usually played the clinging vine, the needy one, while Steve acted distant and independent.

There were occasions, however, when Lynn became angry with Steve and her anger would give her the strength to withdraw from him. At those times, her stone-faced silence would upset and frighten him. His independence was simply an act: a protection and defense against feeling vulnerable. In reality, he was as needy as was Lynn for reassurance and love.

When frightened by Lynn's withdrawal, Steve would become affectionate, try to make conversation, or initiate sex. When Lynn responded to his advances, however, he would begin again to distance himself, and Lynn would return to her usual role of pursuer.

For some couples, the switching of roles is a rare occurrence. For others, there is a constant play back and forth.

Sometimes, both partners manage to play both roles at the same time. Lynn and Steve had both learned the "I'm fine, you're not" scenario early in life. Each of them was very critical of the other and each of them felt very much criticized by the other.

Lynn was verbal in her criticism: She would correct Steve's language, ridicule his taste in dress, and try to change his so-called lower-class political views. She held up her family and the people she worked with at the college as examples for Steve to follow.

Steve, on the other hand, had his own way of putting Lynn down. Without ever saying a word, Steve could make her feel inadequate as a cook by simply frowning at the food on his plate and making a great show of adding salt. He could threaten her self-confidence by ignoring her and flirting with her friends.

When we see how we continually play out the roles in our scenario, we understand how it is that we contribute to our own unhappiness. We grasp, perhaps for the first time, the fact that we choose to play the role we do . . . and that it is possible for us to choose not to play that role. It is possible for us to discard our scenarios entirely.

□□□

The second goal of recovery is healing. We need to heal the wounds of childhood, the wounds inflicted each time we felt neglected, rejected, or abandoned.

We can begin our healing by taking a look at how we understand love. Each of us has a different idea of how love is best expressed. Certain words and behavior "say" love to us, while others do not.

How do we want to be loved? Do we want to be admired?—applauded?—encouraged?—listened to with approval and acceptance? Do we want to be given gifts?—called by an endearing nickname?—hugged or cuddled?

Lynn would have felt loved if Steve had spent more time with her. Steve would have felt loved if Lynn had shown respect for his success in business.

For Reflection: What is it that tells me I am loved?

The behavior that we most desire from a partner is usually the behavior we were denied as children. It is the expression of love our parents withheld from us. It is also the expression of love we withhold from ourselves.

We tend to treat ourselves as our parents treated us. If they were critical toward us, we will tend to be self-critical. If they withheld presents or pleasures, we will probably deny ourselves these things. If they ignored or ridiculed us, we will find it hard to value or trust our own ideas, feelings, or desires.

Lynn wanted Steve to spend more time with her, but she did not value or enjoy her own company. She had few activities, interests, or social life apart from Steve.

Steve wanted Lynn to respect his business ability. But he himself discounted his work as being less valuable than her family's social status or her education. He never spoke with pride of his achievements or celebrated his various successes.

We cannot hope to receive from another person what we do not give ourselves. The relationship we create with our partner is a reflection of the relationship we have with ourselves. We are not able to receive more from a relationship than we already possess.

For Reflection: Do I treat myself as I want another to treat me?

□□□

Our healing comes from changing the way we treat ourselves. By treating ourselves with love, we "reparent" ourselves. We meet the needs we had in childhood that our parents failed to meet. As a result, we develop the self-esteem that is necessary to our emotional health.

With self-love and self-esteem, we become independent of the love and approval of others. We may want love and approval, but we do not need it. We no longer feel it is necessary for our survival. We no longer have to betray ourselves in order to get it.

Ironically, it is when we are no longer desperate for love and approval from others that we receive it. When we like ourselves, enjoy ourselves, accept ourselves with forgiveness and unconditional love, we find others who like us, enjoy us, and give us a forgiving and unconditional love. If we treat ourselves with respect, if we are generous toward ourselves, tolerant of ourselves, we expect and receive similar behavior from others.

To change the way we treat ourselves, we need to change the way we think about ourselves. Our healing involves having a completely new idea about who we are.

Looking at Scripture: Can I effect changes in myself by changing my attitude?

> Do not conform any longer to the pattern
> of this world, but be transformed by the
> renewing of your mind. Then you will be
> able to test and approve what God's will
> is—his good, pleasing and perfect will.
> ROMANS 12:2

Changing what we think about ourselves is difficult. Early parental attitudes toward us are powerful. We not only internalize these attitudes and project them onto other people, we project them onto God. We assume that he feels about us as our parents did. Some of us are so confused and self-destructive, we think it is God's will that we are unhappy. We think we are being selfish if we love or care for ourselves.

Scripture, however, teaches us that God is our perfect parent. Being a perfect parent, God loves us first, before we love him (1 John 4:19). He knows that his love gives us the ability to love ourselves. The commandment that we love others as we love ourselves is based on the assumption that we do love ourselves.

□□□

If you feel the need to work more deeply on the goals of understanding and healing, you will find help in the book that is the second in this series of books: *God, I'm Still Hurting: Break Free from the Legacy of Family Dysfunction.*

God, I'm Still Hurting deals in depth with the origins of codependent behavior. It provides guidelines for looking at the past and understanding current behavior in the light of childhood experiences. Guidelines for healing are also provided, with specific suggestions on how to reparent yourself.

Recovery from codependency is a gradual process that will take time. It is possible for you to work on more than one goal at a time, or to switch back and forth, working on different goals at different times. You can proceed at your own pace, choosing whatever you feel ready for.

□□□

The third and final goal of recovery is growth. Growth is necessary if we are to interact with a partner in new and healthy ways.

Our growth depends, first of all, on acquiring new skills. The next two chapters deal with the communication skills needed to promote intimacy and facilitate problem-solving.

In order to grow, we also need information—information not available to children growing up in a dysfunctional home. In the second part of this book you will find a comparison between codependent and healthy relationships. You will be given a model to follow and an idea of what works.

Looking at Scripture: Do I need information for my growth?

> By wisdom a house is built, and through understanding it is established; through knowledge its rooms are filled with rare and beautiful treasures.
> PROVERBS 24:3–4

□□□

As you reach toward the goals of understanding, healing, and growth, you will begin to see the world differently. You will begin to see choices you do not see now, and you will gain the courage and power to make those choices. You will be free to love and be loved.

CHAPTER 4
Communication and Intimacy

We promote intimacy with our partner by being honest—by revealing our feelings, as well as our ideas, hopes, and dreams. When we share in this way, our own willingness to trust and be vulnerable is likely to be matched by our partner.

Sometimes we have a partner who is unwilling or unable to share feelings. The unwillingness may come from fear or from cultural or childhood restrictions and inhibitions. In some cases, our partner may be emotionally numb because of substance abuse or a compulsive activity such as workaholism. In such cases, we may be unable to establish communication.

Sometimes, however, a partner is unwilling to be honest with us because of the way we have responded in the past. Codependents often sabotage intimacy by responding in a negative way to a partner's self-disclosure.

We think we are being supportive when in fact we are being critical or judgmental. We think we are being helpful when we are actually making our partner feel inadequate by preaching or teaching.

We sometimes offer advice when it is not needed or wanted. Or we offer advice before we have paid attention and responded with care to our partner's feelings.

Below are some comments expressed by Lynn and Steve. Each comment is followed by a series of possible responses from the other person. Each response is then translated into what the original speaker may actually be hearing.

□□□

STEVE'S COMMENT: "When I called Logan today, I found out he wasn't going to renew his contract. I tried to reason with him, then lost my temper. I really blew it."

Response #1:

If Lynn says: "Oh, honey, don't feel bad."

What Steve may hear is: "I'm not willing to deal with your feelings. I expect you to discount or ignore what you feel."

Response #2

If Lynn says: "Well, Steve, that's life. We all get a no sometimes."

What Steve may hear is: "Stop complaining and grow up. You sound like a big baby."

Response #3:

If Lynn says: "It's probably because you've been late on deliveries. Why don't you get a letter out to this man apologizing for the delays and promising better service?"

What Steve may hear is: "I need to teach you how to run your business."

Response #4

If Lynn says: "This is awful. And they've been predicting a recession."

What Steve may hear is: "You have more to worry about than you realize."

Response #5

If Lynn says: "Well, that makes three cancellations so far this year."

What Steve may hear is: "I'm keeping records, and I'm going to add this failure to all the rest."

Response #6

If Lynn says: "You sound so upset. Are you blaming yourself for this?"

What Steve will probably hear is: "I'm interested in and have respect for your assessment of this situation."

Using any of the first five responses, Lynn would probably increase Steve's distress. He might turn on her in anger or he may simply "shut down" and walk away, refusing to discuss the matter further.

Lynn's last response, however, shows interest, concern, and respect. It enables Steve to continue to talk about what he feels and to begin to arrive at how he wants to handle the situation.

□□□

LYNN'S COMMENT: "I found some gray hairs today. And I noticed I'm getting a lot of wrinkles around my eyes. My mother aged early. I'm probably going to look the way she did."

Response #1

If Steve says: "The important thing, Lynn, is the kind of person you are. Beauty is only skin deep."

What Lynn may hear is: "You have a distorted and superficial sense of values."

Response #2

If Steve says: "What did your mother look like?"

What Lynn may hear is: "Your feelings are not of interest to me. Let's talk about your mother."

Response #3

If Steve says: "I don't see any gray hair or wrinkles."

What Lynn may hear is: "If I can't see the problem, it doesn't exist. Ignore your feelings. I will."

Response #4

If Steve says: "Why don't you dye your hair? And buy some wrinkle cream."

What Lynn may hear is: "You really do look bad. Since you probably can't figure out what to do, I'll have to tell you."

Response #5

If Steve says: "You look okay. Have you seen my briefcase?"

What Lynn may hear is: "You and your feelings are unimportant. I'm the important person around here."

Response #6

If Steve says: "Are you worried about getting old?"

What Lynn will probably hear is: "I care about you and what you're going through."

Unlike the first five responses, Steve's last response shows that he is "tuned in" to what Lynn is saying. Lynn is encouraged to confide in him further.

□□□

STEVE'S COMMENT: "Tommy's getting impossible. This morning I told him he couldn't hang out with those boys down the street. He just looked at me like he hated me. What's it going to be like when he's a teenager?"

Response #1

If Lynn says: "All kids his age act rebellious."

What Steve may hear is: "I need to teach you about life."

Response #2

If Lynn says: "Well, I speak to Tommy in a gentle way, and we get along fine."

What Steve may hear is: "You're not a good parent. Pay attention, and I'll show you how to do it."

Response #3

If Lynn says: "Don't worry, I'll talk to him when he gets home tonight. I'll explain to him how you feel."

What Steve may hear is: "This is obviously beyond your abilities to handle. I'll have to step in to see that things are done right."

Response #4

If Lynn says: "Well, I'm having trouble with Lisa. Wait until I tell you what happened with her piano teacher."

What Steve may hear is: "Your problem with Tommy is not important. I want to talk about my problem with Lisa."

Response #5

If Lynn says: "Tommy is growing up fast. Are you worried that things are going to get worse between you two?"

What Steve will probably hear is: "I am trying to put myself in your shoes. I can tell this is something important and I'm here for you if you want to talk more about it."

In her last response, Lynn shows Steve she understands his real concern: that he will grow increasingly estranged from his own son. She opens the door for further discussion.

□□□

LYNN'S COMMENT: "You know, Dad's birthday is coming up, and I told Diana I wanted to give him a trip to Palm Springs. She said I was flaunting my money. I told her she was just cheap, and we really got into it. Anyway, now she says she is never going to talk to me again."

Response #1

If Steve says: "You and your sister have been squabbling since you were kids."

What Lynn may hear is: "This is childish. I can't be bothered with this."

Response #2

If Steve says: "Well, just how much will the trip cost? And what was Diana going to buy?"

What Lynn may hear is: "Never mind how you feel. Give me some information on the argument and I'll decide who was right."

Response #3

If Steve says: "If Diana doesn't want to talk to you, you're better off. She keeps you on the phone for hours and you can't get anything done."

What Lynn may hear is: "I don't want to talk about your problem with Diana. I want to talk about my problem with your not meeting your responsibilities."

Response #4

If Steve says: "Everything happens for the best. You'll look back on this someday and laugh."

What Lynn may hear is: "This is no big deal. I can handle this with a couple of clichés."

Response #5

If Steve says: "You've always been so close to Diana. Are you worried you'll really lose her?"

What Lynn will probably hear is: "I understand how serious this is for you. I'm here to listen if you want to talk about it some more."

In Steve's last response, he allows Lynn to have her feelings without contradicting or dismissing what she is saying. Instead of giving her advice, he encourages her to continue talking so she can arrive at her own solution to the problem.

□□□

In the material above, each original comment expresses some emotional distress. However, we may also respond inappropriately to comments that express pleasure or happiness. Below are some examples.

STEVE'S COMMENT: "I finally found a barber I like. I got this great haircut for half what it used to cost me."

If Lynn says: "Well, those bangs aren't exactly stylish."

What Steve hears is: "My opinion about your hair is more important and more valuable than your opinion."

LYNN'S COMMENT: "My boss told me today what a great job I did on the enrollment report."

If Steve says: "Did he offer you a raise?"

What Lynn hears is: "Praise doesn't mean anything. It's the money that says you're valuable."

STEVE'S COMMENT: "I'm excited about this fishing trip coming up. I haven't seen Gary for years."

If Lynn says: "I just hope I can manage everything while you're gone."

What Steve hears is: "You ought to feel guilty about going off like this."

LYNN'S COMMENT: "I had such fun today teaching Lisa how to bake cookies."

If Steve says: "Is it safe to eat them?"

What Lynn hears is: "If you're the teacher, they probably won't have come out very well."

In the examples above, the responses are all negative and hurtful. They stop the flow of happiness or pleasure expressed in the original comment. Like most of the responses in the earlier sections of this chapter, they show a lack of caring and respect for the speaker.

The best response we can make to a person who is happy or pleased is to acknowledge or share their joy. We can offer congratulations or simply say, "That's great."

□□□

The message we send to another person is not only in the words we use. The expression on our face and the tone of our voice are also important.

For example, here is a question that can suggest very different things to the person listening, depending upon how it is asked: "Why did you do that?" If the question is asked in a cold and demanding tone of voice, here is the message that might be conveyed: "You owe me an explanation. Try to defend yourself, in spite of the fact that I've already passed judgment on you."

If the question is asked in a tone of incredulity, the message that is conveyed is: "I can't believe you did this thing. How could you be so stupid?"

In contrast, it is possible to ask the same question in a warm, supportive and caring way. The message then becomes: "Because I care about you, I am interested in learning about your ideas and your feelings. I believe you to be a smart person who has good reasons for doing what you do."

□□□

When we respond to our partner in a negative way, when we ignore, ridicule, judge or dismiss our partner, all helpful communication comes to an end. We promote distance instead of intimacy—anger instead of love.

Looking at Scripture: How important are my responses to my partner?

> A man finds joy in giving an apt reply—
> and how good is a timely word!
> PROVERBS 15:23

> Pleasant words are a honeycomb, sweet to
> the soul and healing to the bones.
> PROVERBS 16:24

CHAPTER 5

Communication and Problem Solving

The difficulty codependents have in communicating is most apparent when we come into conflict with our partner. Intent on defending ourselves or accusing the other, we seldom share what we feel. Even when shouting or crying, we may be unable to reveal what lies under our anger or hurt.

As we argue, we often lose sight of the original problem or issue. We bring up former problems and complaints, sometimes changing the subject completely. We become involved in a power struggle to determine who is right and who is wrong.

At the same time, we usually stop listening to our partner. We do not want to hear anything that sounds like an attack. We think we know what the other person is saying, has said, and will say. While our partner is

speaking, we are busy planning our reply—or interrupt-
ing.

For Reflection: When in conflict with my partner,
how much do I reveal about what I am feeling? How
well do I listen?

Once our focus is on winning, we are no longer able
to give and receive the information that we need to
resolve our problem. We create a no-win situation.

Regardless of who is finally argued down or shouted
down, regardless of who gives up or holds fast—both of
us lose. Resentment and bitterness widen the distance
between us.

□□□

One of the ways we can avoid no-win arguments is to
enter into problem solving with a genuine interest in
learning what our partner feels and why he or she feels
that way.

Listening to our partner is not the same as agreeing
with him or her. It is possible to understand and accept
feelings and ideas as being appropriate for our partner
and still not accept them as being appropriate for us.

The attitude we need to convey when listening is: "I
know you have good reasons for feeling what you feel
and believing what you believe. You are an intelligent
and sane person. Even if I don't share your feelings or
beliefs, I can understand and I accept how and why you
feel and believe as you do."

Most of the subjects we argue about cannot be proven to be either right or wrong. They are simply a matter of opinion: for example, the best place to spend a vacation or how neat a house should be. On these subjects, we can only respect our partner's feelings and ideas while still honoring our own. *We do not have to prove our partner wrong in order to hold different or opposing ideas.*

We can also listen to, understand, and even sympathize with our partner—and still not comply with what he or she is asking of us. In some cases, we may be unwilling or unable to do what is asked of us. We can still respect our partner's right to ask. *We do not have to prove our partner wrong in order to have the freedom to say no.*

Although our partner may want us to agree or comply, he or she will usually be satisfied with being listened to in a respectful and caring way. Listening well can prevent a disagreement from turning into an angry and hurtful conflict.

Looking at Scripture: How important is listening?

> My dear brothers, take note of this: Everyone should be quick to listen, slow to speak and slow to become angry.
>
> JAMES 1:19

> Do you see a man who speaks in haste? There is more hope for a fool than for him.
>
> PROVERBS 29:20

He who answers before listening—that is
his folly and his shame.

PROVERBS 18:13

□□□

It is important, not only to listen, but to let our partner know we are listening. Listening well includes responding to what our partner says. This requires giving feedback that indicates that we are interested in what is being said.

We can show our interest both by body language and by our verbal response. Body language is especially revealing. If we fidget, look away, grimace, or check the time, we are clearly impatient and intolerant of what is being said. If we are still, keep our eyes on the speaker, and have a friendly expression on our face, we encourage that person.

It is also helpful to repeat back to our partner, in our own words, what it is we have heard. Or we can respond by asking questions: "Are you saying that . . ." "Do you feel . . ." These responses demonstrate our interest and our willingness to understand. They give our partner a chance to change or clarify what has been said.

Responding with reflective statements or questions may be difficult at first. We may feel awkward or foolish when we start to do this. Some discomfort is to be expected, however, when practicing any new skill.

Acknowledging and reflecting feelings is not a trick or gimmick. It cannot be used mechanically. It is helpful only in an atmosphere of honesty, love, and respect.

□□□

When it is our turn to speak, we need to know what we want. It is not possible to be honest with another person until we are first honest with ourselves.

It may not, however, be possible for us to identify our feelings and our wants when we are caught up in a conflict. We may need time, on our own, to think through the answers to the questions below.

What am I feeling?

Sometimes we are so out of touch with our feelings, that it takes a while to find the answer to this question. We may not be able to get beyond feeling sad or angry.

For some of us, sadness is a cover-up for anger, which may seem to be too dangerous, threatening, or disloyal an emotion. In contrast, some of us may be unable to feel anything but anger. Anger may seem to be safer than underlying emotions such as fear or embarrassment. Before attempting to communicate with our partner, it is best to explore and understand our deeper emotions.

Why am I feeling this way?

Sometimes our emotions are affected by our physical well-being. For instance, we may be tired, ill, or worried about our job.

However, when we have intense interpersonal feelings, they are usually connected to past experiences. Our response to a current situation may have a great deal to do with our history—especially our childhood.

The point of understanding this connection with the past is not to minimize or discount our feelings. Rather it is to be able to accept these feelings while gaining a new perspective on our current problem.

What do I want?

It is not reasonable to expect our partner to do something for us that we can do for ourselves. However, when we do want or need something from our partner, it is important to ask for what we want.

We cannot assume that our partner will know what we want without our asking for it. Our wants are based on the unique combination of our personality and our history. We are unique and, to some extent, our wants are unique and cannot be guessed by others.

We usually avoid asking for what we want because of low self-esteem. We may feel undeserving of a yes response and worry that we will then be under obligation to the other person. At the same time, we may be fearful of a no response that we would take personally as a rejection of our very selves.

Being able to ask for what we want, however, is a sign of strength and health. We ask because we value ourselves and are taking care of ourselves.

Before we ask for what we want, it is best to find the answers to some related questions: "How long am I willing to wait for what I want?" "Would I be willing or able to live without this forever?" "What am I willing to do to get what I want?"

Sometimes our wants are unrealistic. They are based on the unmet needs of childhood, and no amount of effort on anyone's part would be enough to satisfy us. However, even when we are uncertain as to how reasonable our request is, it is helpful to recognize the little child within us who feels deprived.

In asking for something, we need to be specific. The following request is too vague: "I want you to spend more time with me." How is the partner to know how much time is enough? It would be better to ask that certain blocks of time be set aside, on particular days, for activities both partners can agree upon. In this way, the request can be negotiated so that both have input and both partners understand exactly the terms of their agreement.

Asking does not mean we will automatically get what we want. There may be reasons why our partner cannot or will not comply (reasons that make sense only to our partner).

☐☐☐

When we have discovered what we are feeling and why, when we know what we want, we are ready to communicate these things to our partner. We express these things without a demand for agreement or compliance. Our attitude is: "This is my view of the situation. You may not be able to agree with me or give me what I want, but you can help me by listening and letting me know you understand."

Since we will be talking about ourselves, the word we will use most often is "I" rather than "you." By talking about ourselves—our feelings and our wants—we can avoid judging, blaming, or criticizing our partner. As a result, our partner will be willing to listen to us instead of preparing a defense or counterattack.

Serious communication should be delayed until both partners have time available. It is helpful to set a "date," agreeing upon the time, place, and length of time for communication. Initially, it may also help to establish some ground rules, such as how long each person gets to speak without interruption.

Honest, caring, and respectful communication will usually bring about a negotiated settlement that is satisfactory to both partners. However, even in those cases where a problem is not totally resolved, this kind of communication produces benefits.

One benefit is that we talk about our feelings. In particular, the expression of our negative feelings helps to relieve or even dissipate those feelings. As we share with our partner the reasons why we feel as we do, our perspective may even change.

There is a benefit, too, in asking for what we want. Regardless of whether we get a yes or no answer, we walk away from the communication knowing we have taken care of ourselves. We have made a statement about our regard for ourselves, and our sense of self-worth.

The most important benefit, however, is that the relationship we have with our partner has been strengthened rather than undermined. Honest, caring, and respectful communication enhances trust and love.

PART II

HOW CAN I TELL IF IT'S LOVE?

CHAPTER 6

Intimacy

Codependent partners are not necessarily abusive, neglectful, or even inconsiderate of one another. In some cases, they may be caring, thoughtful, and considerate. Regardless of how pleasant their relationship may be, however, there is usually little, if any, intimacy.

Intimacy involves letting another person see who we really are. It involves being honest about our vulnerability, our fear, our anger, our defects. We are able to be intimate with another person only if we have a strong sense of self-acceptance.

As codependents, however, we have little self-acceptance. Growing up with abuse or neglect, we have feelings of low self-esteem, even shame, about who we are. We believe that honesty about who we are will inevitably lead to rejection or abandonment.

Because of our fear, we keep our real selves hidden from our partner. Using words, or using silence, we build a self-protective wall to hide behind.

The Sounds of Codependency

LYNN: "I'm very verbal, but not really honest. I mean, I talk a lot to Steve, but there's a lot I cover up with my talking. We've been married for ten years, and there's a lot he doesn't know about me. For instance, I never tell him how jealous I feel when he flirts with other women. Anything I say to him is designed to make me look pretty good.

"When I first met Steve, I told him a lot of very personal history about myself right away. What I told him was basically true, but sort of dramatized for effect. When I told him about some of the other men in my life, I was trying to impress him with how desirable I was to other men. When I told him about my childhood, I was trying to make him feel sorry for me and protective of me.

"I can cry about certain things in front of Steve, but often, when I'm crying, I'm really angry. I'm afraid to show my anger. If Steve does or says something that hurts me, I just go numb. Sometimes I even keep smiling and talking. I don't want to let him see how much power he has over me. If he knew how much I needed him, he'd probably be out the door."

STEVE: "Lynn keeps saying she wants me to talk to her. She got upset with me when my father died because I wouldn't tell her how I felt about it. I just didn't see the point. Anyway, I don't even know what I felt. And I certainly didn't want to get emotional. I don't think Lynn could handle my losing control. Or maybe I couldn't handle it.

"I don't let Lynn know when business is bad. When she sees I'm depressed and asks me why, I just avoid answering. Sometimes I'll let her know I'm angry over losing a contract, but I never let her know that I'm scared—or that I think I might fail. She'd really despise me if she knew how weak I was."

Some of us are so frightened of intimacy that we remain single. We manage to be attracted only to unavailable people, or we manage to find something wrong with any potential partner. If we do get married, we hide in silence, or behind meaningless words, or we keep our distance by being engrossed in our work, our hobbies, or involvement with other people.

For Reflection: In what ways do I avoid intimacy?

□□□

Because we fear intimacy, we not only hold back from our partner, we help our partner to hold back from us. We do what we can to prevent the other person from being honest.

The Sounds of Codependency

LYNN: "I say I want Steve to tell me everything, but I guess I only want to hear what I want to hear. I mean I can't tolerate anything negative. If he starts to tell me anything negative about himself, I always stop him and try to build him up. Isn't it my job to build his ego? If he tries to point out something negative about me, I'll start crying or get sulky and withdraw.

"I also feel threatened if he tells me about problems at work. I get so scared the business might fail—I feel I have to fix things. I usually point out what he's doing wrong and tell him what he needs to do to correct the situation. It makes him so angry, he just doesn't talk to me about work anymore."

STEVE: "I can't stand it when Lynn gets emotional. Even when she's calm, I don't want to hear her start in on some heavy problem. I especially don't want to hear what she thinks is wrong with our marriage. I'm afraid everything is just going to come apart at the seams.

"And also, I feel responsible. Whenever Lynn is angry or depressed, I feel like she's saying it's my fault. Or I think she expects me to fix it. Sometimes I try to handle it, but if she doesn't accept what I say right away, I get impatient. I may start yelling, or just walk away. I guess I make it hard for her to talk to me."

We fear intimacy, not only because we fear being known, but because we fear knowing. We were taught, as children, that negative feelings are dangerous and the truth might ruin everything. So we help our partner to be as "hidden" and emotionally distant as he or she wants to be.

For Reflection: How do I contribute to my partner's holding back from intimacy?

□□□

Without intimacy, we will never feel loved. Even if our partner speaks to us of love, and shows us love, we will not be able to accept it. After all, we tell ourselves, "My partner doesn't know who I am. My partner loves a 'me' that doesn't exist. If my partner knew what I am really like, he or she wouldn't love me."

We need to feel loved, not just for the wonderful things about us, but in spite of our failures and shortcomings. Love can only exist when we are well known to one another, when we are real to one another. It can only exist when we are tested by in-depth contact and in-depth knowledge of the other person. Otherwise, what looks like love is merely courtesy, the good manners we extend to people we hardly know.

If we look at what Scripture says about love, we find that it is demonstrated by certain attitudes and behaviors. Some of these attitudes or behaviors are positive responses to negative situations. They require patience, tolerance, and forgiveness for difficult people and situations that test our love.

Looking at Scripture: What is love?

> Love is patient, love is kind. It does not
> envy, it does not boast, it is not proud. It
> is not rude, it is not self-seeking, it is not
> easily angered, it keeps no record of

> wrongs. Love does not delight in evil but
> rejoices with the truth. It always protects,
> always trusts, always hopes, always perse-
> veres.
>
>   1 CORINTHIANS 13:4–7

We cannot claim to love our partner until we know and accept those things about our partner that we might view as weak or negative. We cannot ourselves feel loved unless our own weaknesses and failings are known and accepted by our partner. Both partners need to give verbal expression to their important feelings, wants, and needs—even when these might possibly upset or even repulse the other person. Without the risk of this kind of intimacy, we cannot know the certainty of love.

For Reflection: Am I willing to know and be known by my partner?

□□□

Codependent relationships tend to move along very quickly. Although we are afraid of intimacy, we also long for it—or at least the illusion of it. So needy are we of an immediate sense of being "connected" that we may enter quickly into sexual activity (the subject of the next chapter). We may also reveal, early in the relationship, personal information that is more appropri-ate for sharing later on.

Some of us commit to financial arrangements or schedule our time in a way that locks us into a relationship before it is wise to do so. It is difficult for us to simply engage in small talk for awhile and let the relationship take its course. We jump in and expose ourselves, putting ourselves at risk, both physically and emotionally, with people we have not yet had time to judge as being trustworthy.

In contrast, a healthy relationship takes time to develop. It begins with "small talk" and with times spent together at work or play. We learn about the other person as we see him or her respond to these shared experiences, to other people, and to us.

Intimacy is further developed by discussion. We talk about our shared experiences, how we feel about them, and how our feelings may change as we listen to one another.

Eventually, we share with one another our personal history. While this recounting may cover some material we are not very proud of, it does not involve a blow-by-blow accounting or a detailed description of everything we have been through. Rather, we share the nature of our past experiences, emphasizing not what happened, but how we felt about what happened.

In a healthy relationship, intimacy grows gradually, over an extended period of time. This is because intimacy depends on trust, and trust can only be developed in time.

We do not trust people because of what they say, but because of how they behave. In particular, we watch how they react to our self-disclosures. We share a little and then check to see how our honesty is received before increasing the amount and kind of sharing. We need to know that what we say will be accepted in a loving way—that our confidences will be kept—and that what we reveal will not be used against us.

Healthy people move very slowly and cautiously in this process, but they do keep moving. They want to build bridges, not walls. Eventually they are able to reveal their most vulnerable selves: negative feelings, fears, inadequacies, as well as hopes and dreams.

□□□

Intimacy grows out of trust and it also increases trust. Intimate partners feel secure even when separated by long distances or for long periods of time. The emotional bond between them protects them from jealous worries or fears.

Intimate partners also feel comfortable when they are together. They do not need to be constantly working on their relationship. When a problem comes up, they use communication skills to resolve their problem, and then they return to their usual state of being relaxed and easy with one another.

Intimacy seems difficult to us codependents and we try to avoid it. Yet it is intimacy that makes life easier and more pleasant. It is through intimacy that we gain a sense of security, comfort, and peace.

CHAPTER 7
Sex

Codependents tend to move into sexual activity very early in a relationship. One reason for this is that sex answers both our need to reach out to and also our need to hide from the other person. Sex provides us with a physical connection that gives us the illusion—but not the risk—of an emotional connection. We call our relationship intimate. We pretend that what we have is love.

Another reason we may rush into sex is that we feel vulnerable in relationships, and we try to protect ourselves by using sex as a means of establishing control. We may believe, for instance, that having sex with someone will enable us to influence that person into becoming more attentive or loving. Or we may believe that sex will enable us to "catch" or to "hold" the other person.

The Sounds of Codependency

LYNN: "I had some sexual experience before meeting Steve, but I never enjoyed it much. When I met Steve, I pretended to be more responsive than I really was. It wasn't the sex I wanted. I just wanted Steve holding me and showing me affection. I always felt so abandoned when he left me. Even if he stayed the night, I felt lonely when he left in the morning."

STEVE: "Sex with Lynn was great in the beginning. Bed was the one place I was completely in charge. It was the one place she never picked on me or got negative. I didn't have to worry about not being good enough for her. I felt powerful in bed. I figured that, with enough good sex, Lynn would get sweeter and more accepting."

Instead of enabling us to catch or hold someone, sex may become a trap that catches us. Most of us cannot become physically involved without also becoming emotionally involved and vulnerable. The other person, sensing our dependency, may become more wary, distant, and unwilling to make a commitment.

We will probably fail, also, if we try to use sex to change our partner. Instead, our sexual involvement may cause us to tolerate behavior that we would not otherwise be willing to overlook. It may lead us to gloss over defects that will eventually cause us serious problems. Since people are on their best behavior in the beginning of a relationship, any shortcomings we notice are probably going to become more pronounced as time goes by.

For Reflection: In what ways have I used sex to try to control or manipulate a partner?

Emotionally healthy people do not need to control or manipulate another person to "make" a relationship happen. They are able to quietly, even passively, allow the relationship to develop or die as seems best. They trust that God is in charge of their lives and whatever happens will be for their best.

□□□

Another problem with relationships in which sex plays an early and primary part is that it becomes more difficult for us to get to know and make rational judgments about the other person. If our initial focus is on sex, rather than on verbal communication, we may never learn who our partner is. Or we may learn too late.

When they met at the party (Chapter 1), Lynn and Steve made assumptions about one another that were completely wrong. Lynn attributed Steve's minimal attempts at conversation to his being self-assured. She had no idea he was afraid of sounding uneducated. She thought his interest in his drink was based on his lack of interest in her. It was a detachment she had seen in her father and that she had labeled as strength. She did not know Steve was drinking to overcome his discomfort at feeling out of place at the party. It never occurred to her to question whether Steve might have a problem with alcohol.

Steve made his own mistakes in assessing Lynn. He assumed that her social poise, her stylish clothes, and her critical attitude all meant that she was self-assured. He had no idea that she questioned her attractiveness and her femininity.

Because their relationship very quickly moved into sexual activity, both Lynn and Steve managed to feel connected and intimate without ever having to risk getting to know one another. In fact, they became unwilling to learn anything about the other person that might threaten their relationship. Lynn never seemed to notice how much Steve drank, or how distant he was when they weren't actually engaged in sex. Steve never seemed to notice that Lynn's interest in clothes was something of an obsession and that she shopped compulsively. He seemed unaware that her sexual passion was a lot less strong than her passion to change and improve him.

For Reflection: In what ways has an early sexual involvement kept me from knowing my partner?

In a healthy relationship, sexual activity does not form a part of the initial process of getting acquainted and developing a relationship. Sexual involvement that could color or distort evaluation of a potential partner is avoided, while the person is assessed as a likely candidate for compatibility, similar beliefs, values, interests, and goals.

□□□

Whether sexual feelings are present at the beginning

of a relationship or grow slowly as the relationship develops, they may be overwhelmingly strong. Even though we may know the pitfalls of sexuality outside of marriage, and may know that God would have us safe from such pitfalls, we may still be tempted.

Many of us, at some point in our lives, find ourselves in the kind of struggle Paul spoke of in Romans 7:19–20. We know what is right, we want to do what is right, and yet, like Paul, we may fail.

Here again, what is needed is both emotional and spiritual maturity. With emotional maturity, we are unwilling to betray our bodies or ourselves by using sex to manipulate, control, deceive, or hide from another person.

With spiritual maturity, we understand that our bodies are sanctified by God. We know we are to honor our bodies.

Looking at Scripture: Why should I honor my body?

> Therefore, I urge you, brothers, in view of God's mercy, to offer your bodies as living sacrifices, holy and pleasing to God—this is your spiritual act of worship.
>
> ROMANS 12:1

> Don't you know that you yourselves are God's temple and that God's Spirit lives in you?
>
> 1 CORINTHIANS 3:16

□□□

If codependents use sex as a substitute for—and a protection against—emotional intimacy, they may never learn to communicate. Even if they marry, they may continue to relate at a superficial level, unable to share and resolve serious problems.

As these unresolved problems grow in number, anger and resentment build. Each partner brings to bed feelings of being misunderstood, unappreciated, or abused. As times goes by, the sex that once served as the primary bond between this couple now becomes a major source of difficulty.

The Sounds of Codependency

LYNN: "When it comes to sex, I don't even want to try anymore. Sometimes I blame Steve—he's so abrupt about it all, and there's never any tenderness. How can I make love if I don't feel he loves me? But then I get to thinking it's all my fault. I just don't seem to be as responsive as the women I read about in books or see in movies.

"Sometimes I think it doesn't work because I'm always pretending it's working. I get so confused and disheartened by it all, I just want to stop having sex altogether. I never say I've got a headache, but I sure use every other excuse."

STEVE: "I was able to put up with Lynn's critical attitude when things were okay in bed—but now she's negative about sex, too. It's gotten to be a real chore. At one point, I couldn't even perform. I was so scared and upset about that, I started fooling around with a woman at the office—just to reassure myself I was still okay."

Lack of communication and the resulting inability to solve problems will inevitably have repercussions in the bedroom. One or both partners may go from enjoying sex to pretending to enjoy sex—or to avoiding it completely. They may in anger or in hurt turn to sexual encounters outside of the marriage. Or they may become sexually dysfunctional.

For Reflection: Have I been in a long-term relationship where sex has become a problem?

□□□

Sometimes codependent couples are unable to identify the problems that underlie their strained sexual relationship. They may even deny there are any problems "except in bed." If they seek counseling in the form of sex therapy, what they discover surprises them.

In most cases, such therapy deals only briefly with instruction about sexual practices or techniques. "How to" information is required by only a small percentage of the couples who seek such counseling. The main focus of the therapy will usually be on teaching the couple how to communicate. Good sex is dependent on good communication.

In a healthy relationship, the partners have established good communication. They are able to trust one another with feelings. They are able to be honest with one another about needs and wants. They say what pleases them and what doesn't. They ask for what they want—without feeling rejected if the partner chooses not to respond. They listen to their partner's feelings, needs, and wants—knowing they, too, have a choice about responding. They do these things in and out of bed.

In the first part of this book, there are two chapters on communication. They might just as easily have come under the single heading of "A Guide to Good Sex." When we achieve emotional intimacy, we feel safe with our partner. The trust that is established enables us to surrender ourselves to sexual passion.

In a healthy relationship, there is a natural ebb and flow to sexual interest, and a decrease in sexual activity is usual during times of emotional or physical stress. There are, however, no serious problems in the bedroom. When communication is good, partners are always discovering new things about one another. The excitement of this discovery is their aphrodisiac. As the years go by, sex becomes more interesting and more fun.

CHAPTER 8
Expectations

Codependents expect a great deal from a relationship, and many of these expectations are unrealistic. One expectation is that our partner will always be loving toward us. We expect our partner to respond to our feelings and our needs as a perfect parent would. We even expect our partner to know our feelings and our needs without our having to verbalize them.

Since we often marry people who are handicapped in their ability to love, we are usually disappointed and frustrated. If we do marry a warm and loving person, we may still be dissatisfied. Having missed so much as children, we seem to need, want, and expect more from an adult relationship than is reasonable.

The Sounds of Codependency

LYNN: "Steve never remembers my birthday. It hurts me to know I have to remind him. And then, though he buys me something, sometimes it isn't even wrapped. And the cards he gives me are always the funny ones, or the sexy ones, not the romantic ones. Last year, he bought me a very expensive necklace and earrings to match. But he just handed it all to me without waiting for a special time. And he didn't say anything special—just 'happy birthday.' I'm always so sad and disappointed on my birthday.

"It's hard for me to believe Steve really loves me when he doesn't seem to take the time or make the effort to show it. It would mean so much to me if he would just surprise me with a phone call in the middle of the day to say he appreciates me and that he's thinking about me."

STEVE: "I don't expect a seven-course dinner every night. I know Lynn works, too. But she seems so uninterested in cooking. She doesn't seem to remember which foods are my favorites. Sure, she's busy and has the kids to take care of. But she finds time to work in her garden. So how come she can forget the laundry? Or the shopping? I get crazy if I find I'm out of my favorite breakfast cereal. If she cared about me, she'd be on top of things.

"And why isn't she more interested in sex? Oh, she goes along with it all the time, but she never takes the initiative or gets wild or playful. She says she loves me, but she doesn't much show it."

Like Lynn and Steve, we may expect our partner to be consistently attentive to our needs and feelings. We may even expect our partner to anticipate our needs or to understand our feelings without our having to express them. When our partner does not or cannot respond, we feel unloved.

For Reflection: Do I often feel disappointed or hurt in a relationship?

Focused on our own needs and feelings, we may be unable to appreciate the needs or feelings of our partner. We may be unable to see a situation from our partner's view point. We may not realize how often we, ourselves, fail to respond to the needs and feelings of our partner.

Looking at Scripture: Are there ways in which I am as unloving as I judge my partner to be?

> "Why do you look at the speck of sawdust
> in your brother's eye and pay no attention
> to the plank in your own eye?"
>
> MATTHEW 7:3

In a healthy relationship, both partners have a high level of self-esteem. As a result, less reassurance is needed. At the same time, these partners find it easy to ask for, and give, the support, encouragement, and nurturing that say "I love you."

In a healthy relationship, both partners also have a strong sense of humility. As a result, there is a greater tolerance for those human failings we are all sometimes guilty of: forgetfulness, short-temper, discourtesy, or neglect.

There is also an understanding that perfect love can be received only from a perfect being, and that being is God. Only God can be to us the ideal parent we want our partner to be. Only he can give us the consistent support, encouragement, and nurturing that convinces us we are loved.

□□□

The second expectation that codependents have is, in a sense, the flip side of our first expectation. Not only do we expect our partner to be our ideal parent, we expect to be this kind of parent for our partner. We think that being in a love relationship means we are supposed to take care of someone.

This caretaking may involve trying to protect, teach, guide, rescue, or improve our partner. We also assume responsibility for whether our partner is happy or unhappy.

Some of us caretake our partner to the extent that we become victimized. We may do this in order to feel good about ourselves. We enjoy being able to complain about all we "have" to do. It is a way for us to win admiration for our saintliness or martyrdom.

Codependents also use caretaking as a way of appeasing a partner: "If I'm good enough to you, if I do whatever you want me to, you won't get angry at me." Or we may use it as a way of becoming indispensable: "If you need me enough, you won't leave me." Most of this, however, takes place at an unconscious level.

The Sounds of Codependency

LYNN: "Steve can't even pick out a handkerchief by himself. I have to go with him any time he shops. Usually I just go by myself to buy his clothes. Even with a good wardrobe, he needs me when he gets dressed to select what goes well together.

"Actually, getting Steve dressed in the morning and out the door is a major operation for me. He ignores the alarm, or goes back to sleep, so I have to be sure I keep an eye on the time and wake him a couple of times. I usually bring his coffee to him in bed, and I try to cheer him up if he's grouchy with a hangover. He's always missing something, and I have to find it for him. Finding his watch in the morning can take me a long time. He never leaves it in the same place twice."

STEVE: "When we first got married, Lynn seemed unable to manage her checking account; nothing was added or subtracted correctly, and she was often overdrawn. She also misused the credit cards. Now I keep tabs on her checkbook and I hold onto the credit cards. I also take charge of her monthly paycheck from the college. I give her a cash allowance each week— even though it means I sometimes have to go to the supermarket because she's spent the money elsewhere and we're out of food.

"I don't talk to her about things like our mortgage or insurance. I take care of all the bills and make all the decisions myself about investments or budgeting. She seems to think money grows on trees."

Codependents seldom realize that they are involved in caretaking. They assume that what they are doing falls under the category of being a good wife or husband. They assume it is a loving, rather than a handicapping thing to do.

For Reflection: In what ways have I "parented" my partner?

In a healthy relationship, partners share responsibilities on the basis of what they are best suited for, what they like to do, and what seems like a fair division of labor. In addition, they do give one another a certain amount of nurturing. They attend to one another's physical needs when sickness, job requirements, or other reasons make it difficult for the partner to be self-sufficient. They do not, however, create or perpetuate a dependency that robs the partner of his or her dignity.

They also give one another emotional support by "being there" for the other person: listening to and expressing understanding of problems or pain. They do not, however, assume responsibility for solving the problems or doing away with the pain. They know that God can provide their partner with the wisdom, power, and love that he or she needs in order to deal with any crisis or sorrow.

Looking at Scripture: Who is best able to help my partner cope with life?

> How priceless is your unfailing love! Both
> high and low among men find refuge in
> the shadow of your wings.
>
> PSALM 36:7

In a healthy relationship, each partner entrusts the other to the care of God. They know that God is the ideal parent for both of them.

□□□

A third expectation that codependents have is that being in love will somehow improve us. We often look for a partner who is "better" than us and who will "fix" us. We expect that being in a relationship with this person will make us smarter, healthier, more mature, or more successful. We may also expect the relationship to give meaning and purpose to our lives. We think our partners can fill any spiritual vacuum we may have.

The Sounds of Codependency

LYNN: "I know I'm smart and successful at my job. But I've never felt confident about my looks. My hair is stringy, I'm too thin, and my mouth is too big. I know men don't find me sexy.

"When Steve and I got married, I felt I had finally 'made it.' He's so good looking. It seemed to me our marriage was proof to the world that I was attractive enough and feminine enough for a man like Steve to want me. I mean he could have had just about any woman he wanted. I get jealous when I see he's attracted to another woman. If he ever left me, I think I'd die."

STEVE: "Lynn's got class. She knows exactly what to wear, what to say—what fork to use. And she's comfortable with famous and socially prominent people.

I'm usually sweating through the parties she enjoys so much. Being married to her, I can almost forget the poor and dirty neighborhood I grew up in. I can believe I belong and fit in with better people."

For Reflection: How have I used my partner's assets to feel okay about myself?

In a healthy relationship, each person can appreciate the other person's talents and abilities without depending on the relationship to give them a sense of self-worth. Each partner is able to appreciate equally his or her own assets.

Each person also feels responsible for developing and increasing whatever talents and abilities he or she has been given. Each works separately to take risks, make discoveries, and achieve goals in emotional and spiritual growth. Much of the excitement and joy in a healthy relationship comes from sharing verbally the experiences of these individual journeys.

Looking at Scripture: Do I have a responsibility for developing the resources God has given me?

> "His master replied, 'Well done, good
> and faithful servant! You have been
> faithful with a few things; I will put you
> in charge of many things. Come and
> share your master's happiness!'"
>
> MATTHEW 25:23

It is God who has given us whatever we can claim as good about ourselves, and it is our privilege and responsibility to make the most of those gifts. When we do so, we enhance the self-worth and self-esteem that is God-given.

□□□

Codependents have yet one more expectation that is unrealistic. We expect the relationship we have with our partner to be the only relationship we need. Having found a partner, we tend to limit our outside activities and the number of other people in our lives. We become increasingly isolated and dependent on our partner, and our perspective becomes increasingly narrow.

The Sounds of Codependency

LYNN: "When I started going with Steve, I just dropped all my girlfriends. If I wasn't actually spending time with Steve, I would be thinking about him, or buying clothes that he might like, or just getting ready somehow to be with him. After we were married, I got friendly with my next door neighbor and I've gotten closer to my sisters, but I never see them if Steve is home.

"Not that we do much together. Even when Steve is home he is usually working. When he does relax, he just wants to watch sports on TV. Sometimes I get hurt because I think he doesn't want to be with me. But then I remember that he really doesn't have anyone else. It's like we feel it's just the two of us against the world, and we don't need anyone else."

STEVE: "Lynn works at a college, and I hate it when she drags me to official functions. I feel left out when she gets into one of these high-brow conversations. It's like I've lost her.

"I don't like it either if I come home and find her gabbing on the phone with her sisters. I can't relate to that social world they talk about. She seems so happy and excited talking to her sisters. Why can't she talk to me like that? How come I'm not enough for her?"

We are apt to become possessive or even jealous because we feel so dependent on our partner. Just as an addict protects his "supply," we want to keep our partner to ourselves. We are often threatened by anyone or anything that could take our partner from us.

For Reflection: In what ways have I made my partner the only important person in my life?

In a healthy relationship, the partners understand that they cannot depend on one another to meet all their needs. Some needs and wants they meet on their own. Others they ask their partner, their friends, or their family to meet. For their primary needs and wants, they turn to God.

The key to a healthy love relationship is that it is balanced. The partners balance private "just-the-two-of-us" time with socially integrated activities, some of which are experienced together, some individually. Time is divided between being alone, being with the partner, or being with friends or family.

Time is also spent with God, who is given the highest priority of all. When partners in a relationship are dependent first upon God, when they feel that he alone is essential, crucial and absolutely necessary for survival, there is an ease in the relationship. There is a comfortable ability to enjoy one another without suffocating one another.

Looking at Scripture: What is my priority to be?

> "But seek first his kingdom and his
> righteousness, and all these things will be
> given to you as well."
> MATTHEW 6:33

There is only one person we must have to survive, and that is God. If we make our relationship with him the priority in our life, many other kinds of enriching human relationships will be given to us.

CHAPTER 9
Commitment

Commitment is a major problem for codependents. We either rush into commitment before it is wise to do so, or we do everything possible to avoid commitment.

Those of us who rush into commitment are doing so out of a desperate need to feel connected. Being codependent, we need another person's love to validate us, to give us self-worth. We may be terrified of being alone.

Often we push for commitment before we have had enough time to assess a potential partner. Knowing little or nothing about the other person, we project onto him or her the qualities and attitudes we want in a mate. We ignore danger signals and potential problems, telling ourselves "it will all work out."

Those of us who avoid commitment may also need to feel connected. Our need, however, makes us feel out of control and vulnerable, so we deny our need. We cling to an illusion of ourselves as independent and self-sufficient.

Sometimes we avoid commitment because we are afraid of making the wrong choice. We want to be sure we are selecting the perfect mate, and we agonize over the possibility of making a mistake.

When it comes to making a commitment, some of us go from one extreme to another. We may be pushing for commitment in a relationship and then suddenly become frightened and want to withdraw. This vacillation may go on endlessly.

For Reflection: How do I deal with the issue of commitment?

□□□

Whatever our feelings about making a commitment, once we are in a relationship, we tend to feel "stuck." Because we feel responsible for our partner's feelings, we are afraid to say "no" when we need to. Because we fear a dissolution of the relationship, we may be unwilling to defend ourselves or to physically withdraw from a dangerous situation.

Having grown up in a dysfunctional family, we may have a distorted sense of what loyalty is. We may have been taught to stand by, protect, defend, and maybe even lie for that member of the family who is most disturbed or most difficult.

The Sounds of Codependency

LYNN: "I suspected Steve was having an affair for a long time before I was able to talk about it to anyone. I felt so ashamed—and so scared. I just wanted to pretend it wasn't happening. Finally I got angry enough to confront him. But instead of saying he was sorry, or promising to break it off, he started yelling at me. I couldn't even figure out why he was yelling—except maybe that he had been drinking. Anyway, I began to feel it was all my fault. I've been afraid to bring up the subject again. I think he's broken it off, but I'm not sure. I'll never be able to trust him again. I try and keep myself together for the kids' sake, but sometimes, when I let myself think about it, I just want to die."

STEVE: "Our debts are enormous, and Lynn keeps buying—stuff we don't need and can't use. She's done the most incredible things, like borrowing huge sums from family and friends without telling me. Last week she cashed in some bonds she found in the house and took the kids to Hawaii for a few days. I just can't trust her. I've got a serious cash-flow problem in my business and I'm beginning to think I might go under. I'm worried to death, and sometimes I think I'm going crazy."

If we find ourselves in relationship with a person who is chemically addicted or compulsive, emotionally disturbed or abusive, we usually accept our situation. We may complain about our lot, but, being codependent, we don't make any changes. We seem unable to protect or defend ourselves, to stop or withdraw from the abuse.

In some cases, our inability to act is based on attitudes we developed as children: "This is the way life is supposed to be." "If I'm being mistreated, I must deserve it." "I can put up with anything and still survive."

For Reflection: Why have I tolerated behavior that is harmful to me?

□□□

Sometimes we continue in an abusive relationship because we think it is noble of us to do so. We may look on our suffering as being redemptive—as a sign of our "sacrificial love."

Allowing another person to be abusive or even unkind is not, however, sacrificial love. It is not even love. Love in its highest expression seeks the spiritual health and growth of both the person who is loved and the person who loves. Sacrificial love benefits both the receiver and the giver. Jesus, the perfect example of sacrificial love, gave up his life for the good of others, that they might be saved, and he did it for the joy that lay ahead for him (Hebrews 12:2).

There is a sense in which husband and wife are truly "one flesh" (Genesis 2:24). That which is good for one, is good for the other. That which is bad for one, is bad for the other.

Lynn's allowing Steve to continue in adultery, and to verbally abuse her in the process, did not contribute to his spiritual health and growth. Steve's allowing Lynn to threaten the family's financial security did not contribute to her spiritual health and growth.

The suffering these two endured could not come under the heading of "sacrificial love." Lynn and Steve allowed themselves and their children to endure intolerable situations because they were codependent. They were driven, not by love, but by need, low self-esteem, and fear.

They may have thought they were supporting one another. In fact, they were supporting one another's illness and their own codependency.

For Reflection: How has my tolerance for an unhealthy situation enabled my partner to continue in his or her harmful behavior?

□□□

In a healthy relationship, commitment and loyalty are conditional. Each partner respects his or her own values and beliefs and refuses to disregard or violate these for the sake of the relationship.

A good example of this in Scripture is Abigail (1 Samuel 25:2–42). When Abigail's husband refuses to give provisions to David and his men, Abigail herself rides out to the men with gifts of food. She knows the men have protected her husband's flocks in the wilderness. She knows David is offended by her husband's refusal and has threatened destruction to her family. She wants to honor David's request for these reasons and also because she believes him to be a man of God.

Abigail opposes her husband in a situation where it is appropriate to oppose him. She follows her own understanding of what is right.

When we marry "for better or for worse," we are pledging to give physical and emotional support when times get bad. These "worse" times, however, refer to circumstances that are beyond our control: for instance, accidents or illnesses that cause disability, job layoffs or natural catastrophes that cause economic ruin. If recurring bad times are created or chosen by one partner, loyalty and commitment from the other partner may not be appropriate.

□□□

LYNN AND STEVE: After eleven years of marriage, Lynn and Steve were thinking of breaking up. Their history together involved so much betrayal, distrust, anger, and hurt that they were scarcely able to speak to one another. Their bitterness and unhappiness created serious problems for their two young children who were frightened by the much-discussed possibility of divorce.

It was Steve's drinking that brought matters to a head. Driving home late one night from a local bar, he crashed into another car and came close to killing an elderly couple. For the second time, Steve was convicted of drunk driving, and his sentence this time included mandatory treatment for alcoholism.

During the month Steve spent in the hospital treatment center he received individual counseling, counseling with Lynn, and family counseling with Lynn and the children. For the first time, members of the family began to understand and discuss the problems they faced.

Steve's program of recovery was based on participation in Alcoholics Anonymous. When Steve left the hospital, he continued his weekly meetings in AA. Although a lifelong atheist, he learned in those meetings to turn his life and his will over to a "Higher Power."

In the meantime, Lynn, because of her mother's abuse of prescription medicine, joined a group called Adult Children of Alcoholics. These ACA meetings helped her to return to the faith of her childhood. Eventually Lynn, Steve, and the children began going to church, which met their spiritual needs.

Along with their spiritual growth, they worked on their emotional growth. For almost a year, both Lynn and Steve spent time in individual counseling with a therapist knowledgeable about adult children from dysfunctional families. Each of them discovered there was a great deal to work on besides the problems of addiction and compulsion that had created such havoc in their lives.

Lynn and Steve are no longer in individual counseling, but they are continuing in counseling as a couple. They have come to accept equal responsibility for their marital problems, and they are working together to try to solve them.

It is not a smooth or easy process for them, and sometimes they revert back to fighting or withdrawing. Twice they have reconsidered divorce. These difficult times, however, are becoming fewer in number and farther between.

The next chapter shows Lynn and Steve using the communication skills they learned in counseling. You will see from this example how communication can be used to resolve conflicts and promote intimacy.

CHAPTER 10
Lynn and Steve in Recovery

Lynn and Steve had been in counseling for about a year when they were invited to a dinner party by the dean at Lynn's college. During dinner, Steve became absorbed in conversation with the pretty and vivacious young woman seated next to him. Later, when everyone had moved into the living room, Steve continued his conversation with this woman.

Lynn had been watching Steve all evening, and by the time they were in the car driving home, she had become cold and withdrawn. Steve tried to make conversation, but she did not respond, and finally he, too, fell silent.

Although she was quiet, her body almost numb, Lynn's mind tracked back and forth through Steve's offenses: his past affair, his insensitivity to her, his betrayal of her, his disregard for her feelings. She rehearsed to herself different opening lines: "Well, it looks as though you don't have to be drinking to make a fool of yourself." "Have you and Connie chosen a motel yet?"

They had argued about this issue so much in the past that she could easily imagine Steve's reaction. She could picture the set of his jaw and hear him yelling: "You're impossible. What do you want from me? If you think I'm going to stop talking to half the human race, you're crazy."

After all the work they had put into saving their marriage, would it end anyway? Lynn tried to think about what she and Steve had learned in counseling. What was she supposed to do now? She couldn't remember. She closed her eyes. "Oh God," she prayed, "please help me. I hate him. I can't think. What should I do?"

Steve interrupted her prayer. "What's eating you, anyway?"

Lynn took a deep breath and tried to control her voice. "I'm not feeling too great. But it's late and I'm tired as well as confused, so it's probably not a good time to talk. I'd like to talk tomorrow, though—maybe after work."

Steve thought he knew what was upsetting Lynn and he did not want to talk about it. At the same time, however, he was relieved that she sounded calm, and he had learned from experience that their planned talks worked well for both of them. Although he was always anxious at the start and sometimes wanted to bolt out the door, he would feel good about the results. "Tomorrow night's okay. Just don't jump on me the minute I get home from work. How about after dinner?"

"That's fine. But I don't want to feel rushed because of a TV show you want to watch. I'd like to have at least an hour set aside, even if we don't need all that time. How about 8 to 9?"

By the next day, Lynn felt less upset about the party. At lunchtime she found privacy in the empty room behind her office and she began to prepare for the talk that night. Although not as upset, she still found it difficult to think logically. Her feelings would well up and her mind drift off. Finally, by writing down her thoughts, she came to some clarity about what she was feeling, why she was feeling that way, and what it was that she wanted from Steve.

Lynn went over to the door and locked it. She then got on her knees, something she had not done since she was a child. "Lord, I'm so frightened of saying these things to Steve. And I'm not even sure I understand what I've written here. Please give me courage tonight—and wisdom, Lord. Help me talk to him without accusing him or making judgments. Please give me the right words to say."

At 8:00, Lynn and Steve were seated facing one another. They had gone into the den for privacy and had told the children they couldn't be disturbed for an hour. Lynn began, in a shaky voice, by asking Steve to let her talk for about 10 or 15 minutes. "Some feedback will be okay, though, because it would help me to know you understand what I'm saying.

"I got upset last night at the party watching you with Connie. Maybe it was reasonable for you to be talking to her as much as you did—and maybe I overreacted, but I did feel jealous."

Lynn could no longer keep looking at Steve. Her eyes went down to the floor. "I was jealous, but it was more than that. I felt humiliated. I felt as though somehow I were being compared to Connie, and that everyone at the party, my boss and coworkers, could see that you found her more attractive than me." Lynn hesitated, her throat burning as she tried to hold back the tears. Her voice was breaking as she went on. "I know I'm not very pretty, and Connie is, and now I'm showing my age, and she's so young."

Steve looked at Lynn sitting in her chair. Her shoulders rounded, tears on her cheeks, she had lost her usual air of self-assurance. He had been prepared for one of her nastier attacks and had come into the conversation feeling hard and defensive. He felt the muscles in his face relax now as he gave her feedback. "You felt you were in competition with Connie?—and that you were losing?"

"Well, yes, but not just losing in the sense of losing to Connie—but really losing you. I mean, I know you are working on the marriage, but sometimes I still feel I'll lose you.

"You know that Dad was away from us a lot, and it wasn't just because of his deployments overseas. I told you about his affairs. Once, when I was ten, he packed up and left to live with another woman for about a year. Even after he came back, I knew he was cheating on Mom, or at least I thought so. I was always thinking he'd leave us. I kept trying to figure out what was wrong with me that he'd want to leave." Lynn was sobbing by now. "I keep waiting for you to leave, too."

Steve was surprised. Although Lynn had spoken before of her father's infidelity, it was always with sarcasm. She had never revealed to him how painful it was for her. He wanted to comfort her, to say something helpful, but felt uncertain and even confused at his own strong feelings. Lynn said she needed some tissues and left the room to get them. When she returned she was calmer and began talking again.

"I understand that you need to feel free to interact socially with women. I know that a lot of this is my own problem that I have to deal with. When we're at a party, though, it would help me if you could give me some attention—or show me some affection. If you could come up to me during the evening and say something nice, maybe just 'I love you.' Or hug me and tell me I'm looking good. I think that would help me relax and let go of you during the evening."

By this time, Steve wanted to be helpful. He agreed to doing what he could when they were out with other people. "I wouldn't feel comfortable hugging you—you know I'm not that way in public, but I will say something nice to you during the evening."

"Thanks." Lynn took a breath and went on. "There's another thing, too, I want to ask of you. From what you've said in counseling, I know that you're sorry about the affair you had—that you think of it as a big mistake. I want to ask you, though, to tell me now that you'll be faithful to me. I just want to hear you say it out loud."

Steve hesitated. He felt uncomfortable at the idea of making a formal declaration. Why couldn't Lynn be satisfied with his comments in counseling? Then he remembered what she had told him about her childhood, and it seemed reasonable for her to ask. "I promise you, Lynn, that I'll be faithful to you."

Lynn felt comfort and relief at hearing Steve say these words. When he leaned forward and reached out his hands to her, she leaned forward too and put her hands in his. Steve lifted her hands and kissed each one.

After a moment, Steve rose and moved away to the window. Lynn leaned back again in her chair, suddenly realizing how tired she felt. She was quiet, thinking. She had supposed their communication was over, but after some moments of silence Steve began to speak.

"You know, I do talk to the women more than to the men at these parties. I feel less awkward with them. The men are these egghead professors, and I feel dumb." Steve paused. His heart had begun to pound, and he started speaking quickly. "I told you I had some courses at a junior college. But that wasn't true. I didn't graduate from high school—I just couldn't make it through that last year." He stopped to catch his breath, and wait for his heart to quiet. His next words came slowly. "These college parties are awful for me—especially now that I'm not drinking."

Lynn was looking at Steve in amazement. She tried to think of some feedback to give him, but before she could speak, he went on.

"The women are smart, too, but I know they're attracted to me, so it doesn't matter if I don't sound so good. I know they're interested in me—and they keep the conversation going, so it's easier for me."

"Is that why you're drawn to the women?"

"Well, yes, but it's not just that." Steve had been watching her carefully as he spoke, but now he looked away. "Maybe, too, I've known that you get jealous." He looked back at her. "But I didn't realize how hard that was for you. I just liked knowing I was important to you."

He stuffed his hands into his pockets, his fists clenched. "You know, it's hard for me, living up to your standards. Sometimes I get angry and want to leave, but most of the time I wonder how much longer you're going to put up with me. I wonder when you're going to kick me out."

Lynn got up from her chair and walked to Steve. As she approached him his hands softened and came out of his pockets. "I love you, Steve. All I want is for us to work things out so we can be happy together." Steve felt her cheek, cool and wet against his own as they wrapped their arms around one another.

This conversation happened after Steve and Lynn had been in therapy for about a year. During that time, they had been practicing, in planned talks like the one above, the skills that enabled them to be as direct and honest as they were.

Their communication did not completely resolve the issues discussed. Lynn still had to deal with her childhood fear of betrayal and abandonment. Steve still had to deal with his sense of inadequacy and his need to seek self-worth in the eyes of other women. However, in sharing honestly about these things, some of the power was taken out of Lynn's fear and Steve's need. Steve's social interaction with men and women became somewhat more balanced, and Lynn's reaction to his behavior more tolerant.

They were able to sustain their relationship during this time of growth because they had found a new understanding of one another and a new trust in one another. Communication had enabled them to turn an ongoing problem into an opportunity for strengthening their marriage.

□□□

In learning to communicate with our partner, we learn to love in a deeper and more satisfying way than we may have thought possible. We love one another, not because of how wonderful we both are, but in spite of how flawed we both are.

Our spiritual growth is affected by our ability to love in this way. As we undergo the testing, healing, and learning required to love our partner, we grow in our ability to love God.

In the Bible, the same Hebrew word for love is used to describe the spiritual relationship existing between God and his people and the romantic relationship existing between King Solomon and his Shulamite bride. In whatever context we learn to love, we draw closer to God and to his purpose for us.

Looking at Scripture: How important is love?

And now these three remain: faith, hope
and love. But the greatest of these is love.
1 CORINTHIANS 13:13

GUIDELINES FOR GROUPS

Meetings

1. If possible, choose a quiet meeting place where there are no distractions such as phone calls or children needing attention. Many churches, banks, and businesses make rooms available to groups free of charge.

2. At the first meeting, give each person a few minutes to explain why he or she has joined the group. Emphasize, though, that no one has to share who does not feel ready to do so. Volunteer to begin by telling your own story. After going around the group, return to anyone who has not spoken and ask gently if he or she is ready to talk yet.

3. You may want to follow the tradition of other self-help groups and have people give their first names only. This tradition helps underscore the confidentiality of the sharing.

4. During the meeting, members may take turns reading from this book. Any member of the group may then comment on the reading, or share a personal response. A chapter may be covered in one meeting, or it may take several meetings, depending on the discussion generated.

5. Begin and end each meeting with prayer, asking the Lord for wisdom and encouragement. You may want

to follow the tradition of other self-help groups and have the group members join hands for the closing prayer.

6. Meetings should start and end promptly. One to one-and-a-half hours should be sufficient. Allow time at the end of the meeting for any necessary business.

7. Avoid discussion of religious or denominational differences, of various kinds of therapies, or other issues that could result in debate or divisiveness.

8. Do not allow eating, smoking, or drinking during the meeting, as these distract from the business at hand and may be a problem for compulsive over-eaters or people with addictions to nicotine or caffeine.

9. Provide the group with a list of members' names and phone numbers, and encourage people to call one another during the week for "mini-meetings."

10. Some members may benefit from attending more than one meeting a week. They can be encouraged to join a Twelve-Step group such as Codependents Anonymous (See "Other Resources").

11. If your group begins to grow beyond ten or twelve members, you may want to start a second group. Small groups are best because they encourage an intimate level of sharing and everyone gets a chance to share.

12. When you have finished going through this book,

you may want to begin again with Chapter 1. As you study the material again, you may find yourself relating to it at a new and deeper level. It is often difficult for us to understand and accept certain ideas until we are progressing in our recovery.

Group Interaction

The guidelines that follow will help create an environment of trust, safety, and support in your group. They should be read aloud, and discussed, at the first meeting. It will also be helpful to review them occasionally, especially if new members join after the group has started.

1. Assure Confidentiality: Everything we hear in our meetings should be kept confidential. No member of this group is ever discussed outside of this group, not even with another group member. Our healing is dependent on the trust we have in one another, and the freedom we feel to share openly and honestly, without fear of exposure outside of the meetings.

2. Avoid Cross-talk: Cross-talk is talking to another person about their problems rather than discussing our own. It is all right to refer briefly to what another person has said, but each of us needs to talk about our own experiences, feelings, or problems. For instance, you could say: "I felt upset when you talked about your father hitting you, because last week I . . ." We must be especially careful to avoid cross-talk that involves criticism, advice, or denial of another person's pain.

a. Criticism: If we feel criticized or judged, our response will be to stop sharing, and we will experience an increased sense of guilt, hopelessness, and isolation. We need to be free to admit certain personal negative things knowing that the response of the group will be loving acceptance. (The only exception to the "no criticism" rule is when a member says or does something that violates the guidelines of this group. Such behavior is subject to discussion and group decision.)

b. Advice: We tend to resist advice, often because it leaves us feeling "talked down to." Sometimes we feel that the advice is given without understanding or sympathy for the particulars of our personality, our history, and our situation. Even when we know the advice to be good, we may feel powerless to follow it. As a result, even good advice may leave us feeling hopeless. We are able to learn and grow from receiving love, support, and acceptance and from seeing others getting well. What we share here is not advice, but our own experience, strength, and hope.

c. Denial of Negative Emotions: It is important that each of us feels free to express negative emotions such as pain, grief, or anger. Much compulsive behavior is the result of not being "in touch with" our feelings or being afraid to acknowledge or express those feelings. We should never cut another person off with a statement such as, "You're forgetting the Lord can bring good out of this" or "You have to have faith that this will work out." Such statements are true, but they are not helpful when used to cut a person off from expressing feelings. If anything, they create more distress by their implication that the person suffering is lacking in faith and is somehow not a good Christian. When our feelings are discounted we feel invalidated. We stop sharing our feelings, and we lose all hope of working through and being freed from our pain.

Leadership

Being a group discussion leader does not require professional training. You are not expected to have all the answers. You are not asked to teach. If you are willing to work on your own problems, if you do so with honesty, humility, and vulnerability, you will set the best possible example for the group.

Being a group leader does not mean you are responsible for anyone's getting well. Recovery from compulsive behavior is a difficult process that can often take a very long time, and that may be marked by severe setbacks or relapses. It is not your job to correct, improve, or heal anyone. That is the job of the Lord, and he works when we are ready and willing for him to do so.

To sum up, the leader's job is not to teach or to heal, but to serve. There are four ways to serve your group:

1. Help provide a loving, trusting environment.

2. Maintain a balance between time spent reading from this book and time spent in sharing.

3. Work on your own problems.

4. Pray for the members of your group during the week.

Ideally, leadership should be rotated with each meeting, so that all members share this service.

OTHER RESOURCES

Information on Codependents Anonymous (CODA) groups may be obtained from:

Codependents Anonymous, Inc.
P.O. Box 335777
Phoenix, AZ 85067

The books below deal with various aspects of developing an intimate relationship. Some deal specifically with codependency.

Covington, Stephanie. *Leaving the Enchanted Forest: The Path from Relationship Addiction to Intimacy*. San Francisco: Harper & Row, 1988.

Larsen, Earnie. *Stage II Relationships: Love Beyond Addiction*. San Francisco: Harper & Row, 1987.

Norwood, Robin. *Women Who Love Too Much: When You Keep Wishing and Hoping He'll Change*. New York: Simon & Schuster, 1985.

Paul, Jordan and Margaret Paul. *Do I Have to Give Up Me to Be Loved by You?* Minneapolis: Compcare Publications, 1983.

Woititz, Janet. *Struggle for Intimacy*. Pompano Beach, Fla.: Health Communicators, 1985.

Also by Claire W.

GOD, HELP ME STOP!
Break Free from Addiction and Compulsion

Here is a presentation of the Twelve Steps of Alcoholics Anonymous as applied to any addictive or compulsive behavior: alcoholism, overeating, smoking, compulsive gambling, sexual addiction, etc. Verses from the Bible illuminate each step of emotional and spiritual healing. Includes the author's personal story of recovery.

"We have used *God, Help Me Stop!* in a group therapy context, as well as for clients in individual therapy, and it is very helpful in both settings. Thank you for your part in such a practical, Christian approach to the problems of dependency and addiction."

—Ruth Blight, Counselor
Counseling Group, Burnaby, B.C.

"*God, Help Me Stop!* has really helped me in my struggle against alcoholism—I've been sober three months now. Thank you for a wonderful tool to work with."

—V.C., New Boston, MI

"As one involved in health ministry, I recommend this workbook to those in the pastoral ministry, as well as anyone working with clients who are ready to take the first step to recovery."

—Stoy Proctor
Ministry: International Journal for Clergy

Also by Claire W.

GOD, I'M STILL HURTING
Break Free from the Legacy
of Family Dysfunction

Times and places change, but the painful experiences and feelings of childhood may be endlessly recreated in adulthood. Here is a Bible-based approach to emotional healing for anyone who has grown up in a dysfunctional family. Questions for reflection and suggested writing assignments make the recovery process personal and powerful.

"We used *God, I'm Still Hurting* in a group study where it helped many to see that biblical truth and emotional healing go hand in hand. One member said, 'I've been hurting all my life—a slow death. This material helped me see the other side, the side of the living and personal God whom I could finally call my loving Father.' Personally, I have found tremendous insights into the healing of fear and guilt carried since childhood. One cannot help but be touched by the sincerity and simplicity of the truths presented in this book."

—Pat Klose, Pastor
Sabre Springs Community Church
San Diego, CA

"In *God, I'm Still Hurting*, we discover 'the anger which covers our hurt, the hurt which covers our fear, and the fear which covers our grief.' The author shows us the value of these feelings and how to turn them into resources for emotional and spiritual growth."

—Lee Hanna, Psy.D.
Marriage, Family & Child Counselor
Ramona, CA

Books by Claire W. are available in both book and workbook format. You may buy books at your local Christian bookstore or by calling 1-800-727-3480. To order workbooks, please see order form at back of book.

Also by Claire W.

GOD, HELP ME CREATE
Realize Your Creative Potential

Whether you want to start a business or write a novel . . . design a building or develop a hybrid rose . . . here is a simple, Bible-based guide to help you start, keep at, and complete the creative project of your choice.

"Claire W. challenges the raw gems of creativity that lie buried within us. Like a diamond cutter, she uses her gentle, precise words to carve out potential, chip away at flawed thinking and motives, and help us to uncover and enjoy the many facets of our God-given abilities. Those of us who have worked our way through these pages have increased in value."

—Susan Lenzkes, Author and Lecturer
San Diego, CA

"Here, our secrets are exposed, our dreams revealed, our failures forgiven, and our gifting affirmed and channeled."

—Judith Dupree, Poet
La Mesa, CA

ORDER FORM

The God Help Me Series
is also available in the following formats:
Workbooks: 8½" x 11", with space to enter Scriptures and comments.
Audio Tape Sets: 2 tapes, 2 to 3 hours listening time, unabridged text.

	Workbooks	*Tape Sets*
GOD, HELP ME STOP!	_____	_____
GOD, I'M STILL HURTING	_____	_____
GOD, WHERE IS LOVE?	_____	_____
GOD, HELP ME CREATE	_____	_____

Total Number of workbooks _____ @ $12.95 $_____

Total Number of tape sets _____ @ $14.95 $_____

Shipping and Handling on first item $ 4.00_____
    on _____ additional items @ 50¢ each $_____

Sales Tax only on shipments to California: 7.25%
    (San Diego County: 7.75%) $_____

TOTAL $_____

Method of Payment:

[   ] Check or money order to Books West

[   ] Visa   [   ] MasterCard

Card # | | | | | | | | | | | | | | | | | |

Expires | | | |

Signature _____

VISA/MasterCard Phone Orders: 1-800-253-8641

Name _____ Phone _____

Organization _____

Street _____

City_____ State_____ Zip_____

BOOKS WEST / P.O. BOX 27364 / SAN DIEGO, CA 92198